Other Books and Series by Jeff Bowen

Applications for Enrollment of Chickasaw Newborn Act of 1905
Volumes I thru VII

Cherokee Intermarried White 1906 Volume I thru X

Applications for Enrollment of Creek Newborn Act of 1905
Volumes I thru XIV
Applications for Enrollment of Choctaw Newborn Act of 1905 Volumes I thru XX

Choctaw By Blood Enrollment Cards 1898-1914 Volumes I thru XX

Oglala Sioux Indians Pine Ridge Reservation 1932 Census Book I

Oglala Sioux Indians Pine Ridge Reservation Birth and Death Rolls 1924-1932
Book II

Visit our website at **www.nativestudy.com** to learn more about these
and other books and series by Jeff Bowen

Other Books and Series by Jeff Bowen

Compilation of History of the Cherokee Indians and Early History of the Cherokees by Emmet Starr with Combined Full Name Index

1901-1907 Native American Census Seneca, Eastern Shawnee, Miami, Modoc, Ottawa, Peoria, Quapaw, and Wyandotte Indians (Under Seneca School, Indian Territory)

1932 Census of The Standing Rock Sioux Reservation with Births And Deaths 1924-1932

Census of The Blackfeet, Montana, 1897- 1901 Expanded Edition

Eastern Cherokee by Blood, 1906-1910, Volumes I thru XIII

Choctaw of Mississippi Indian Census 1929-1932 with Births and Deaths 1924-1931 Volume I
Choctaw of Mississippi Indian Census 1933, 1934 & 1937, Supplemental Rolls to 1934 & 1935 with Births and Deaths 1932-1938, and Marriages 1936-1938 Volume II

Eastern Cherokee Census Cherokee, North Carolina 1930-1939 Census 1930-1931 with Births And Deaths 1924-1931 Taken By Agent L. W. Page Volume I
Eastern Cherokee Census Cherokee, North Carolina 1930-1939 Census 1932-1933 with Births And Deaths 1930-1932 Taken By Agent R. L. Spalsbury Volume II
Eastern Cherokee Census Cherokee, North Carolina 1930-1939 Census 1934-1937 with Births and Deaths 1925-1938 and Marriages 1936 & 1938 Taken by Agents R. L. Spalsbury And Harold W. Foght Volume III

Seminole of Florida Indian Census, 1930-1940 with Birth and Death Records, 1930-1938

Texas Cherokees 1820-1839 A Document For Litigation 1921

Starr Roll 1894 (Cherokee Payment Rolls) Districts: Canadian, Cooweescoowee, and Delaware Volume One
Starr Roll 1894 (Cherokee Payment Rolls) Districts: Flint, Going Snake, and Illinois Volume Two
Starr Roll 1894 (Cherokee Payment Rolls) Districts: Saline, Sequoyah, and Tahlequah; Including Orphan Roll Volume Three

Cherokee Intruder Cases Dockets of Hearings 1901-1909 Volumes I & II

Other Books and Series by Jeff Bowen

Indian Wills, 1911-1921 Records of the Bureau of Indian Affairs
Books One thru Seven
Native American Wills & Probate Records 1911-1921

Turtle Mountain Reservation Chippewa Indians 1932 Census with Births & Deaths, 1924-1932

Chickasaw By Blood Enrollment Cards 1898-1914 Volume I thru V

Cherokee Descendants East An Index to the Guion Miller Applications Volume I
Cherokee Descendants West An Index to the Guion Miller Applications Volume II (A-M)
Cherokee Descendants West An Index to the Guion Miller Applications Volume III (N-Z)

Applications for Enrollment of Seminole Newborn Freedmen, Act of 1905

Eastern Cherokee Census, Cherokee, North Carolina, 1915-1922, Taken by Agent James E. Henderson
    Volume I (1915-1916)
    Volume II (1917-1918)
    Volume III (1919-1920)
    Volume IV (1921-1922)

Complete Delaware Roll of 1898

Eastern Cherokee Census, Cherokee, North Carolina, 1923-1929, Taken by Agent James E. Henderson
    Volume I (1923-1924)
    Volume II (1925-1926)
    Volume III (1927-1929)

Applications for Enrollment of Seminole Newborn Act of 1905 Volumes I & II

North Carolina Eastern Cherokee Indian Census 1898-1899, 1904, 1906, 1909-1912, 1914 Revised and Expanded Edition

1932 Hopi and Navajo Native American Census with Birth & Death Rolls (1925-1931) Volume 1 - Hopi
1932 Hopi and Navajo Native American Census with Birth & Death Rolls (1930-1932) Volume 2 - Navajo

Western Navajo Reservation Navajo, Hopi and Paiute 1933 Census with Birth & Death Rolls 1925-1933

Cherokee Citizenship Commission Dockets 1880-1884 and 1887-1889 Volumes I thru V

CENSUS OF THE SIOUX AND CHEYENNE INDIANS OF PINE RIDGE AGENCY 1896 - 1897 BOOK 1

TRANSCRIBED BY
JEFF BOWEN
NATIVE STUDY
Gallipolis, Ohio
USA

Copyright © 2021
by Jeff Bowen

ALL RIGHTS RESERVED
No part of this publication can be reproduced
in any form or manner whatsoever
without previous written permission from the
Copyright holder or Publisher.

Native Study LLC
Gallipolis, OH
www.nativestudy.com

Library of Congress Control Number: 2021912853

ISBN: 978-1-64968-120-1

Book cover: "The Great Hostile Camp" 1891, Photographer: John C. H. Grabill; Bird's-eye view of a Lakota camp (several tipis and wagons in large field)--probably on or near Pine Ridge Reservation.
All photos including the one for the book cover are complements of the Library of Congress.

Made in the United States of America.

This two book set is dedicated to
Larry Butts
the deepest and kindest of kindred souls.

TABLE OF CONTENTS

List of Illustrations	vi
Introduction	vii
Census Instructions	xiii
Instructions To Enumerators	xiv
Census of the Sioux and Cheyenne Indians, 1896	1
Recapitulation	2
Wakpamini District	3
Porcupine District	27
Wounded Knee District	47
Medicine Root District	81
White Clay District	105
Pass Creek District	137
Errata	157
Census of the Sioux and Cheyenne Indians, 1897	159
District Totals	161
Wakpamini District	169
Porcupine District	191
Wounded Knee District	211
Medicine Root District	243
White Clay District	269
Pass Creek District	301
Index	323

LIST OF ILLUSTRATIONS

1.	A Cheyenne Warrior of the Future	lxiii
2.	Cheyenne Young Woman	lxiv
3.	Eagle Feather and Baby	lxv
4.	Iron Shell	lxvi
5.	John Lone Bull	lxvii
6.	Pine Ridge Picture	lxviii
7.	Seven Sioux School Children	lxix
8.	Sioux Carlisle Arrival 1879	lxx
9.	White Face	lxxi
10.	Young Oglala Girl	lxxii

INTRODUCTION

The Pine Ridge Agency or now known as the Pine Ridge Reservation wasn't always at its present location nor was it always known as the Pine Ridge Agency. Originally called the Red Cloud Agency it was established during 1871 and situated at the North Platte River close to Fort Laramie, in the southeastern part of Wyoming or Cheyenne Country.

The agency had as their charges mainly the Oglala Band of Lakota at that time but in 1873 relocated to the White River close to Camp Robinson in Nebraska where later the daring escape of the Northern Cheyenne under Dull Knife and his people would take place in January of 1879. "At almost the same time that the board at Fort Robinson rendered and approved its findings and adjourned, an elderly man and his wife and son, the older two in wretchedly bad condition and suffering the effects of cold and long starvation, appeared in the doorway of a cabin near New Red Cloud Agency at Pine Ridge, Dakota Territory. The old man was Dull Knife: Morning Star to his people. Miraculously, they had endured ten days with little or no food as they hid in the freezing grotto among the bluffs west of Fort Robinson before finally breaking away as the soldiers focused along Hat Creek Road, northwest of the post. Around January 19, apparently while most of the soldiers remained to the west, Dull Knife and his wife, Pawnee Woman, and their son, Bull Hump, set out under the veil of darkness, circumventing Fort Robinson as they traced the forested gullies and breaks adjoining Crow Butte and trekked north-northeast toward Pine Ridge Agency, sixty-five miles away. They bypassed Camp Sheridan en route, moving at night and avoiding where possible snow-covered terrain that might expose their passage. Faced constantly with starvation, they consumed dried roots and berries, even gnawed their rawhide moccasin soles for meager sustenance in their dilemma.

After perhaps eighteen days (on February 6 or 7) Dull Knife and his little entourage appeared in the night at the dwelling of Gus Craven, a white man married to a Lakota woman. Dull Knife had known Craven years earlier. There the chief and his party found food and rest as well as assistance to the reservation home of William Rowland, interpreter at Pine Ridge and father of James Rowland, the interpreter at Fort Robinson. From that domicile they at last reached the lodge of Little Big Man, the Oglala leader who had gained notoriety in the events attending the killing of Crazy Horse at the Fort less than two years earlier. "They were very cold and had no clothes on and no blankets," Little Big Man said. "The old man shivered a great deal as he talked to me, and asked to come in to the fire and warm himself. I took pity on him, gave him something to eat, some clothes, two pair of moccasins and all my blankets." There at Pine Ridge, under the aegis of Little Big Man and other caring Oglalas, Dull Knife and his surviving family found seclusion and relief in a lodge along Wounded Knee Creek among other Northern Cheyenne arrivals only a short distance from the agency."[1]

The agency once again during 1877 would once more change its geography and settle on the Missouri River where it intersects with Medicine Creek in what is

---

[1] January Moon; Pgs. 165-166 Para 1-2.

today South Dakota, then one year later finally finish its journey to White Clay Creek and assume the title of the Pine Ridge Agency.

At what point is it that the Cheyenne initially collaborated with the Sioux? It's hard to say. We get different opinions from several sources as to when the Cheyenne first had the use of horses. You can read and some will say they first had contact with the Spanish and Coronado that was the 1500's, there by learning about the horse. Some say in the 1820's when they started coming down from their woodland homes in the Great Lakes area. Yet you find the Cheyenne wondering west before that, spoken of by Lewis and Clark. Grinnell says the Sioux taught the Cheyenne how to dress and cut the buffalo hide yet some historians mention when the Cheyenne settled on the plains there weren't many Sioux bands present. We know the Cheyenne language is of Algonquian descent while the Sioux language is of Siouan descent yet the name Cheyenne is a Sioux word, "Shaiena," more or less meaning, "people who speak in a strange tongue." We have dozens of historical accounts where the Cheyenne fought side by side with the Arapahoe as well as the Sioux. With so much time gone by and those that knew the true story gone also it's difficult to say for sure and yet we know they've had a fascinating and yet treacherous history to be sure.

We know both the Cheyenne and Sioux from early times traveled from woodland settings in the Great Lakes country to the Plains and totally changed their lifestyles. They both wore very similar clothing and had cultures that were somewhat aligned. In early times they both had permanent structures they lived in and weren't totally hunters and gatherers but had an agricultural background to supplement their diets. The Sioux, "Pushed out by the Ojibwa from their ancestral woodlands home near the headwaters of the Mississippi in northern Minnesota, the displaced Lakota began migrating west and reached the heart of the Great Plains about 1760. By the early years of the nineteenth century, they had become superior horsemen, skilled hunters and fierce warriors, commanding a huge section of the northern plains that at one time stretched from the Missouri River of South Dakota to Montana's Big Horn Mountains."[2] At one time, the Oglala were one of the most vast and able-bodied among the seven Teton bands or subtribes including the Brule, Sans Arc, Hunkpapa, Miniconjou, Blackfeet or Blackfoot and Two Kettles as well as being confederated with the Cheyenne.

From George Bird Grinnell's writings he quotes others earlier than himself with statements like this, "Long-continued inquiry among the Cheyennes reveals no account of any wars with those tribes which we commonly called Sioux--that is, the southern branches of the Dakota group. Carver speaks of the Cheyennes as camped in 1766 with the Nadouwessi of the Plains; Trudeau, 1795, speaks of Sioux as associated with the Cheyennes; and Henry, 1806, speaks of Sioux and Arapahoes as in company with the Cheyennes when they visited the Hidatsa to make a binding peace with them.

---

[2] The Dull Knives of Pine Ridge; Pg. 4-5 Para. 7.

The western Sioux today declare that they have always been friends of the Cheyennes, and Rev. T.S. Williamson says, as previously stated, that the Cheyennes "have ever since [their first meeting] been counted a part of the Dakota nation."[3] The Cheyenne and Sioux it seems from their first acquaintance one day near a crystal clear stream or one fall among the yellow leaves of the quaking aspens immediately became friends and family.

Even with their great numbers and tribal confederations they couldn't hold back the destruction of their mostly peaceful existence. Their life sustaining abundance of food and many uses of the buffalo during the late 1700's to the mid 1800's was about to be destroyed by those coming from the east bringing with them what was thought to be civilization. The buffalo from early times were estimated at 50 million but by the 1870's they were decimated by fur traders and next by hired railroads' private armies of extermination. Then came the government policies of destroying Sioux individualism by finishing off the food supply by having the Army slaughter helpless animals that provided economic stability to the Sioux and Cheyenne people. The buffalo wasn't just food for a plains people, the buffalo provided skins for tipis, clothing, moccasins, bedding, saddle covers, and sinew for bow strings, even a buffalo tongue could be used as a hair brush. The use of the buffalo for both the Sioux and Cheyenne as well as other tribes was literally unlimited.

The buffalo was a way of life for the people and they watched it disappear before their very eyes just so they could be controlled and have their lands stolen. Treaties that weren't going to be honored anyway were soon to become a thing of the past. Old chiefs like Black Kettle who wanted to honor their word with the Great White Father had their camps raided without provocation by soldiers and officers with cannons and rifles. One day after thinking he and his people were safe and forming a treaty hew would wake up to screams from his people and the smell of fear in the air. While trying to signal to the soldiers riding down on his loved ones he stood there waving a piece of paper, "the treaty" he had every intention of honoring and believing the lodges in his charge would have peace and serenity for a lifetime. Then to his horror and in his final moments he would witness the slaughter of his people, not only his warriors but the innocent women and children and then finally his own death from a soldier's bullet.

The treaties from the past, just like the one Black Kettle waved above his head, weren't ever going to be honored and the politicians knew it. The treaties that had been written, both past and present, were just a form of deception to eventually make a people think everything was going to be ok while all along planning to cheat them out of everything they owned, not only their land but their way of life. The treaties and the words written upon them were always worthless because there wasn't a stipulation made that was honest or a promise that was meant to be kept. Finally one

---

[3] The Cheyenne Indians History and Society Volume I; Pg. 22 Para. 2.

day even a treaty couldn't be sought after to give the Sioux or Cheyenne any form of assurance of keeping what was theirs or having peace in their lives because, "Surprisingly influenced by religious groups, President Grant signed into law in 1871 the most radical part of his new Peace Policy: abandonment of the treaty system, henceforth denying Indian tribes independent-nation status."[4]

Over the years the Sioux have had to contend with many struggles also, one such event was the massacre of Wounded Knee during December of 1890 and, "On the morning of December 29, the U.S. Cavalry troops went into the camp to disarm the Lakota. One version of events claims that during the process of disarming the Lakota, a deaf tribesman named Black Coyote was reluctant to give up his rifle, claiming he had paid a lot for it. Simultaneously, an old man was performing a ritual called the **Ghost Dance**. Black Coyote's rifle went off at that point; and the U.S. Army began shooting at the Native Americans. The Lakota warriors fought back, but many had already been stripped of their guns and disarmed.

By the time the massacre was over, more than 250 men, women, and children of the Lakota had been killed and 51 were wounded (4 men and 47 women and children, some of whom died later); some estimates placed the number of dead as high as 300."[5]

This material was taken from Indian Census Rolls 1885-1940 (M595) Roll 367. Also found within these pages can be read an original report called, "INSTRUCTIONS TO ENUMERATORS." Concerning the Eleventh Census of the United States, June 1, 1890. Especially interesting is starting at the last paragraph of page nine, "SPECIAL ENUMERATION OF INDIANS." On page 23, number 6 explains Age at nearest birthday which would account for some of the age figures used in this present series such as, Age range 0-6 or 3-6 referring to months. Also it was felt that this document could be used in other genealogical endeavors to explain the way certain censuses have be assembled as far as professions, school attendance, illiteracy, language spoken, mental and physical defects, etc.

From the History of South Dakota, https://history.sd.gov/Archives; underneath in quotes; It should be noticed as mentioned earlier about the dissolution of all Native Americans treaty rights, as understood from this statement, "as long as the grass grows and the water runs these treaties will be honored," [paraphrased] were worthless. The Native People, no matter the tribe, would have honored their word. The creators of the treaties never would. The website given above provides the following explanation below,

"Indian Census Rolls, 1886-1942 (M595). Because Indians on reservations were not citizens until 1974, nineteenth and early twentieth century census takers did not count Indians for congressional representation. Instead, the U.S. government took special censuses in connection with Indian treaties, the last of which was in 1871. The

---

[4] The Northern Cheyenne Exodus in History and Memory; Pg. 32 Para. 1.
[5] Wounded Knee Massacre; Wikipedia.

result of many treaties was to extinguish Indian ties to land. Typically, the Indians agreed to reduce their landholdings or to move to an area less desired for white settlement. Some treaties provided for the dissolution of the tribes and the allotment of land to individual Indians. The censuses determined who was eligible for the allotments. These census rolls were usually submitted each year by agents or superintendents in charge of Indian reservations, as required by an act of July 4, 1884. The data on the rolls vary to some extent, but usually given are the English and/or Indian name of the person, roll number, age or date of birth, sex, and relationship to head of family. Beginning in 1930, the rolls also show the degree of Indian blood, marital status, ward status, place of residence, and sometimes-other information. For certain years – including 1935, 1936, 1938, and 1939 – only supplemental rolls of additions and deletions were compiled. Most of the 1940 rolls have been retained by the Bureau of Indian affairs and are not included in this publication."[6]

What's interesting is the very land where many of these Native Peoples were given to live and own were found out to be flourishing with gold, silver, copper, asphalt, oil and later as needed for weaponry and immense forms of energy, uranium. Creating a new form of want and greed and more deception of what again belonged to these people that just wanted to be left alone.

It's the hope of this author that this work honors those mentioned within these pages and honors their descendants who face new sets of problems each day of their lives simply because promises couldn't be kept a couple hundred years ago and still affects them today.

Jeff Bowen
Gallipolis, Ohio
NativeStudy.com

---

[6] Pine Ridge Agency; p. 19, para. 1-2

Census Instructions

INSTRUCTIONS

(A) A separate roll is to be made of each reservation; also, of each *rancheria* or reserve, and a separate roll of Indians allotted on the public domain or homesteading. The roll is to be based on enrollment and not on residence.

(B) Persons are to be listed by families alphabetically; that is, not only by the first letter of the surname, but also by the second and subsequent letters, when the first letter or letters are the same. For example: Abalon, Abbott, Abcon, Abend, Abiet; Ball, Bell, Bill, Boll, Bull; Carley, Carmen, Carton, etc. Families having the same surname are also to be listed in this way, e. g.: Brown, Anson; Brown, Bill; Brown, Charles; Brown, David. In the case of English translations of Indian names, such as John *Flying-Elk*, Flying-Elk is the surname and is to be listed under F. In such cases the first word of the translated Indian name determines the alphabetical position. The best way to accomplish this will be to write the names of each family group on a separate card; then, arrange the cards alphabetically and type the names therefrom onto the census roll.

Members of a family are to be listed in the following order: Head, first; wife second; then children, whether sons or daughters, *in the order of their ages;* and lastly, all other relatives and persons living with the family who do not constitute another family group.

Annuity and per capita payment rolls are also to be prepared in the same manner.

(C) A family is composed of the following members:
1. Both parents and their unmarried children, if any, living with them; all other relatives and persons living with the family who do not constitute another family group.
2. Either parent and the unmarried children, if the other parent is dead; all other relatives and persons living with the family who do not constitute another family group.
3. A single person over 21 years of age, not living with a relative.

(D) For each person the following information is to be furnished:
1. NUMBER.—A number is to be assigned in serial order. Thus, the first person listed is to be numbered as "1," the second, as "2," and so on until the census is completed.
2. NAME.—If there are both an Indian and an English name, the allotment or annuity roll name is to be given. First, the last or surname; then, the given name in full. Ditto marks are to be used under the surname of the head for the surnames of the other members of *one* family.
3. SEX.—"M," for male; "F," for female.
4. AGE AT LAST BIRTHDAY.—Age in completed years at last birthday is to be shown. For infants under 1 year, age in completed months, expressed as twelfths of a year. Thus, 3 months as $\frac{3}{12}$ yr.
5. TRIBE.—Care is to be taken that tribe, not band or local name, is given. Thus, Ute tribe, not Pahvant, which is a band of Ute. Likewise, Hupa tribe, not Bear River, which is a local name for the members of the Hupa tribe living near Bear River.
6. DEGREE OF BLOOD.—"F," for full blood; "$\frac{1}{4}$+," for one-fourth or more Indian blood; "−$\frac{1}{4}$," for less than one-fourth Indian blood.
7. MARITAL STATUS.—"S," for a single or unmarried person; "M," for a married person; and "Wd," for widowed of either sex.
8. RELATIONSHIP TO HEAD OF FAMILY.—The head, whether husband or father, widow or unmarried person of either sex, is to be designated as such. For the other members, the appropriate term which designates the particular relationship the person bears to the head is to be used.
9. RESIDENCE.—
    (a) At *jurisdiction* where enrolled: Yes or no. The term jurisdiction includes all reservations and public domain allotments under the agency.
    (b) Or at another jurisdiction. The name of the jurisdiction is to be given.
    (c) Or elsewhere:
      1. Post office: Both the proper name of the post office and the class by which it is known (city, town, village, etc.) are to be given. Thus, Lewiston, city.
      2. County.
      3. State.
10. WARD.—Yes or no. Wardship depends primarily upon the ownership of individual property held in trust or upon membership in a tribe living on a Federal reservation. See Circular 2145.
11. ALLOTMENT, ANNUITY, AND IDENTIFICATION NUMBERS.—"Al," for allotment; "An," for annuity; and "Id," for identification, before the appropriate number or numbers. All numbers are to be shown.

(E) Rolls not prepared in strict conformity with the above instructions will be returned for correction.

[7-994.]

Eleventh Census of the United States.
JUNE 1, 1890.

INSTRUCTIONS TO ENUMERATORS.

Under the Provisions of the Act of Congress
approved March 1, 1889.

DEPARTMENT OF THE INTERIOR,

CENSUS OFFICE.

WASHINGTON:
GOVERNMENT PRINTING OFFICE.
1890.

GENERAL INSTRUCTIONS.

DEPARTMENT OF THE INTERIOR,
CENSUS OFFICE,
Washington, D. C., May 1, 1890.

Under the provisions of the act entitled "An Act to provide for taking the Eleventh and subsequent censuses," approved March 1, 1889, a census of the population, wealth, and industry of the United States is to be taken as of June 1, 1890. By the provisions of section 19 of said act the enumeration must be completed on or before the first day of July, and in any city having over ten thousand inhabitants under the census of 1880 the enumeration must be taken within two weeks from the first Monday of June.

One hundred and seventy-five supervisors of census, one or more to each state and territory and the District of Columbia, have been appointed by the President, by and with the advice and consent of the Senate.

APPOINTMENT OF ENUMERATORS.

Upon the approval by the Superintendent of Census of the persons designated for appointment as enumerators in each district the supervisor will issue to each person so named a commission, signed by said supervisor and approved by the Superintendent of Census, authorizing and empowering him to execute and fulfill the duties of an enumerator in accordance with law, and setting forth the boundaries of the subdivision within which such duties are to be performed by him. Accompanying the commission will be a blank form of oath or affirmation [7–062], as required by section 8 of the act of March 1, 1889.

As soon as the commission and printed form of oath are received by the enumerator the receipt of the commission should be acknowledged to the supervisor on form 7–792, and the oath duly subscribed, in accordance with the instructions printed thereon, and transmitted to the supervisor before the first Monday of June, the date fixed by law for the commencement of the enumeration. These requirements must be strictly complied with, as no enumerator is qualified by law to enter upon his

(3)

4   INSTRUCTIONS TO ENUMERATORS.

duties until he has received his commission and filed his oath with the supervisor for his district. It is also provided by law that the enumerator, by accepting his commission and qualifying thereunder, binds himself to carry the work on to completion, unless incapacitated by sickness from so doing. For neglect or refusal to perform the duties required of him under the law he will be deemed guilty of a misdemeanor, and be liable upon conviction to a fine not exceeding five hundred dollars. An enumerator can not throw up the work, therefore, simply because of dissatisfaction or indolence.

DUTIES OF ENUMERATORS.

It is the duty of each enumerator, after being duly qualified as above, to visit personally each dwelling in his subdivision, and each family therein, and each individual living out of a family in any place of abode, and by inquiry made of the head of such family, or of the member thereof deemed most credible and worthy of trust, and of such individual living out of a family, to obtain each and every item of information and all the particulars required by the act of March 1, 1889. All of this data is to be obtained as of date June 1, 1890.

In case no person shall be found at the usual place of abode of such family, or individual living out of a family, competent to answer the inquiries made in compliance with the requirements of the act, then it shall be lawful for the enumerator to obtain the required information, as nearly as may be practicable, from the family or families, or person or persons, living nearest to such place of abode. The term "individual living out of a family" is explained in the special instructions concerning Schedule No. 1 (page 20).

It is the prime object of the enumeration to obtain the name and the requisite particulars as to personal description of every person in the United States, except Indians not taxed.

COURTESY ON THE PART OF ENUMERATORS.

It is the duty of an enumerator, in the exercise of his authority to visit houses and interrogate members of families resident therein, to exercise courtesy and consideration. A rude, peremptory, or overbearing demeanor would be an injustice to the families visited, and would render the members of those families less disposed to give information with fullness and exactness, and would seriously retard the census work.

On the other hand, it is not necessary that the enumerator should enter into prolix explanations or give time to anything beyond the strictly necessary work of interrogation. The enumerator should be *prompt, rapid, and decisive* in announcing his object and his authority and in making his inquiries, but in so doing he should not arouse any antagonism or give any offense.

THE OBLIGATION TO GIVE INFORMATION.

It is not within the choice of any inhabitant of the United States whether he will or will not communicate the information required by the census law. By the fifteenth section of the act approved March 1, 1889, it is provided:

That each and every person more than twenty years of age, belonging to any family residing in any enumeration district or subdivision, and in case of the absence of the heads and other members of any such family, then any representative of such family, shall be, and each of them hereby is, required, if thereto requested by the Superintendent, supervisor, or enumerator, to render a true account to the best of his or her knowledge of every person belonging to such family in the various particulars required by law, and whoever shall willfully fail or refuse shall be guilty of a misdemeanor, and upon conviction thereof shall be fined in a sum not exceeding one hundred dollars.

Enumerators are cautioned, however, not to obtrude unnecessarily the compulsory feature of the enumeration. It will be found very generally that the persons called upon to give information will do so without objection or delay. It is only where information required by law is refused that the penalties for non-compliance need be referred to. The enumerator will then quietly but firmly point out the consequences of persistency in refusal.

FALSE STATEMENTS.

It is further to be noted that the enumerator is not required to accept answers which he knows or has reason to believe are false. He has a right to a true statement on every matter respecting which he is bound to inquire. Should any person persist in making statements which are obviously erroneous, the enumerator should enter upon the schedule the facts as nearly as he can ascertain them by his own observation or by inquiry of credible persons.

6   INSTRUCTIONS TO ENUMERATORS.

This matter becomes of special importance with reference to the statements made concerning members of families who are mentally or physically defective. The law requires a return in the case of each insane, feeble-minded, idiotic, blind, or deaf person, or such as may be crippled, maimed, or deformed. It not infrequently happens that the persons interrogated are disposed to conceal, or even to deny, the existence of such infirmities on the part of members of their household, especially as regards children. In such cases, if the fact is personally known to the enumerator, or if ascertained by inquiry from neighbors, it should be entered on the schedules the same as if obtained from the head or some member of the family.

In the same way the enumerator is not bound by any statement concerning the values produced in agricultural or other occupations which he knows or has reason to believe to be false; also, regarding homes and farms which are reported as having no incumbrances resting upon them, no statement should be accepted which he believes to be false. His duty is to report the actual facts as nearly as he can ascertain them.

PENALTY FOR DISCLOSING INFORMATION.

By the thirteenth section of the act of March 1, 1889, it is provided that "any supervisor or enumerator who shall, without the authority of the Superintendent, communicate to any person not authorized to receive the same any information gained by him in the performance of his duties, shall be deemed guilty of a misdemeanor, and upon conviction shall be fined not exceeding five hundred dollars."

The intent of this provision is to make the answers to all the inquiries confidential, and to prevent disclosures of information which would operate to the personal detriment or disadvantage of the person supplying the same. It is not within the discretion of the supervisor or enumerator to make public or give out for his private use or that of any other person any part of the information obtained by him. All requests, whether from newspapers, local officials, or individuals, for the total population of his subdivision, or other matters pertaining to the enumeration, should be referred to the Census Office for reply. The returns will be tabulated in this office without delay, and the correct

INSTRUCTIONS TO ENUMERATORS. 7

official figures supplied as soon as ascertained. Furthermore, it should be the duty of the enumerator to state, in all cases where objection is raised, that the names and residences will not be used in the printed reports, nor will any statement be made concerning the business or operations of individual establishments.

FALSE OR FICTITIOUS RETURNS.

The law (section 13) further provides:

If he (supervisor or enumerator) shall willfully or knowingly swear or affirm falsely, he shall be deemed guilty of perjury, and, on conviction thereof, shall be imprisoned not exceeding three years, and be fined not exceeding eight hundred dollars; or, if he shall willfully and knowingly make false certificates or fictitious returns, he shall be deemed guilty of a misdemeanor, and, upon conviction of either of the last-named offenses, he shall be fined not exceeding five thousand dollars and be imprisoned not exceeding two years.

By this provision the enumerator is placed under severe penalties to do the work required of him honestly and conscientiously. The boundaries of the subdivision allotted to each enumerator are clearly defined in his commission, and it is his duty to make a thorough and systematic canvass of the territory assigned to him, visiting each house and establishment in order and obtaining complete and truthful returns concerning each individual living or doing business therein, as required by the law and his oath of office.

THE SCHEDULES OF INQUIRIES.

The schedules to be used by the census enumerators are as follows:

Schedule No. 1, relating to population.

Schedule No. 2, relating to agriculture.

Schedule No. 3, relating to general manufactures, and special schedules relating to particular industries.

Schedule No. 5, relating to persons who have died during the census year.

Supplemental Schedules Nos. 1 to 8, relating to persons mentally or physically defective, crippled, maimed, or deformed, or temporarily disabled by sickness or disease; also to homeless children, prisoners, and paupers.

Special Schedule, relating to surviving soldiers, sailors, and marines in the war of the rebellion, and widows of soldiers, sailors, and marines of that war.

8   INSTRUCTIONS TO ENUMERATORS.

In the exercise of the authority conferred on the Superintendent of Census by section 18 of the act of March 1, 1889, Schedule No. 4, relating to social statistics, has been withdrawn from the enumerators.

By the same section it is also provided that, in the discretion of the Superintendent, the mortality schedules and the general and special schedules for manufactures may be withheld from the enumerators, as explained in the special instructions relating to these schedules.

The schedules, in number deemed sufficient for the enumeration, will be sent by the supervisors of census to the enumerators by registered mail. A portfolio is provided for carrying the schedules needed for each day's work. The extra supply of schedules should be left at home in some safe place, and at the completion of each day's work a new supply sufficient to answer the wants of the next day should be placed in the portfolio, and the completed work carefully retained at home in the same order in which the enumeration is made from day to day.

It is expected that the enumerators will prosecute their work at all times with diligence and dispatch. The limitations as to the time in which the enumeration shall be completed make it the imperative duty of enumerators to so arrange their work as to finish within the time allowed by law. An ordinary day's work should cover at least ten hours, and it will often be the case that the enumerators will find it profitable to do considerable work during the early part of the evening. When the work can be prosecuted to advantage there is no objection to such an arrangement on the part of the enumerators.

THE PLAN OF ENUMERATION IN INSTITUTIONS.

The statistics of population and other special data concerning persons residing in institutions will be taken by institution enumerators; that is, some official or other trustworthy person connected with the institution, who will be appointed specially for the purpose.

This plan of enumeration will not be extended to all institutions, but the appointment of special institution enumerators will be determined partly by the size of the institution and partly by its nature.

INSTRUCTIONS TO ENUMERATORS. 9

For those institutions where this plan of enumeration is to be carried out the enumerators for the districts in which such institutions are located will have no responsibility.

Each enumerator will receive in advance of the enumeration due notification from the supervisor for his district as to the institutions which are not to be taken by him. It should be the duty of the enumerator, however, if there is any institution in his district, whatever may be its size or character, to satisfy himself by personal inquiry of the officer in charge whether a special institution enumerator has been appointed, and if not, to proceed to enumerate the population as in the case of all other houses visited by him. On the other hand, if a special institution enumerator has been appointed for it, then it has been withdrawn from his district, and he will leave it to be enumerated by the special institution enumerator.

SOLDIERS AND SAILORS.

All soldiers of the United States army, civilian employés, and other residents at posts or on military reservations, will be enumerated in the same manner as has been provided for institutions, by the appointment of a special resident enumerator; and in all such cases where the district enumerator has been so notified such posts or military reservations should not be included as a part of his district. For posts not garrisoned, and any other posts not so withdrawn, the district enumerator will make the necessary inquiries, and if no special enumerator has been appointed he will include the residents of such posts as a part of his district equally with other elements of the population.

In a similar way all sailors and marines stationed on vessels and at the United States navy yards, as well as resident officers, with their families, will be specially enumerated and need not be taken by the district enumerator if, upon inquiry or by notification, he knows that such special provision has been made.

SPECIAL ENUMERATION OF INDIANS.

The law provides that the Superintendent of Census may employ special agents or other means to make an enumeration of all Indians living within the jurisdiction of the United States, with such information as to their condition as may be obtainable, classifying them as to Indians taxed and Indians not taxed.

10   INSTRUCTIONS TO ENUMERATORS.

By the phrase "Indians not taxed" is meant Indians living on reservations under the care of government agents or roaming individually or in bands over unsettled tracts of country.

Indians not in tribal relations, whether full-bloods or half-breeds, who are found mingled with the white population, residing in white families, engaged as servants or laborers, or living in huts or wigwams on the outskirts of towns or settlements, are to be regarded as a part of the ordinary population of the country, and are to be embraced in the enumeration.

The enumeration of Indians living on reservations will be made by special agents appointed directly from this office, and supervisors and enumerators will have no responsibility in this connection.

Many Indians, however, have voluntarily abandoned their tribal relations or have quit their reservations and now sustain themselves. When enumerators find Indians off of or living away from reservations, and in no wise dependent upon the agency or government, such Indians, in addition to their enumeration on the population and supplemental schedules, in the same manner as for the population generally, should be noted on a special schedule [7-917] by name, tribe, sex, age, occupation, and whether taxed or not taxed.

The object of this is to obtain an accurate census of all Indians living within the jurisdiction of the United States and to prevent double enumeration of certain Indians.

Where Indians are temporarily absent from their reservations the census enumerators need not note them, as the special enumerator for the Indian reservation will get their names.

ENUMERATORS' DAILY REPORT CARDS.

Two postal cards for each working-day of the period allowed for enumeration will be furnished to each enumerator, one [7-761] adressed to the supervisor of his district, and the other [7-762] addressed to the Superintendent of Census at Washington.

The cards addressed to supervisors are printed on gray paper, and those addressed to the Superintendent of Census on buff paper.

On the back of these cards is a printed form for a statement by the enumerator of the number of persons, farms, etc., enumerated by him during the day to which the report relates, and also a statement of the time actually and necessarily occupied in this service.

INSTRUCTIONS TO ENUMERATORS. 11

The enumerator will, at the close of each day, fill up and sign this report. If he is in the immediate neighborhood of a post-office on the following day he will deposit these cards in the mail; if not, he will hold them until such time as he has an opportunity, without undue trouble, to deposit them; but he will not on any account fail to make out and sign the reports of daily work at the time required.

As these reports will be used in determining the compensation of enumerators, it will be desirable for them to exercise great pains in this particular.

In those districts where the enumeration must be made in the first two weeks of June the working days actually allowed by law number twelve, and end with June 14. In a few districts it may happen that the time required to complete the enumeration will exceed this limit, and to cover such emergencies daily report cards are supplied for June 16, 17, and 18. The enumeration must be completed, however, within two weeks in all districts, wherever possible, and the necessity for using these additional cards must be avoided, except for unusual causes only.

Accompanying the daily report cards are two forms of certificate of completion of enumeration, which read as follows:

I certify that on the —— day of ———, 1890, I completed the enumeration of the district assigned me, and that the returns have been duly and truthfully made in accordance with law and my oath of office.

—— ——,
Enumerator for District No. ——.

As soon as the work in each district is finished the enumerator should date, sign, and mail both of these cards, one of which [7-763] is to be sent to the supervisor and the other [7-764] to the Superintendent of Census.

Blanks are also provided for the use of enumerators in making consolidated statements of the time actually and necessarily occupied each day in the prosecution of their work. Upon this form [7-794] should be entered the number of hours and minutes worked each day as recorded on the daily report cards at the close of each day's service, including the time occupied by enumerators in securing from physicians the corrections of the statements of the causes of deaths on Schedule No. 5, in hunting up delinquents and absentees, and in securing information omitted upon their first rounds.

INSTRUCTIONS TO ENUMERATORS.

RETURN OF SCHEDULES TO SUPERVISORS.

When the work in an enumeration district is finished all the schedules not used, together with the portfolio, should be neatly packed and returned in the same package with the completed schedules. The schedules and portfolio should be placed between the two pieces of mill-board provided for their protection and securely tied, and then wrapped in heavy manilla paper in the same manner as when received by the enumerator. The wrapping paper on the package, as originally sent, if preserved and turned (when necessary) will form a suitable cover for the return of the completed work.

The label [7-696] bearing the printed address of the supervisor is to be used by enumerators for the return of the schedules, and should be pasted on the outside of the package and over the old label bearing the name and address of the enumerator (if the wrapping paper is not turned). This label has the word "registered" stamped thereon, and by attaching the same to the package of schedules it can be sent to the supervisor to whom addressed by registered mail. In signing registry receipts the enumerators are cautioned in all cases to add their official title to their names.

COMPENSATION.

By the eleventh section of the act of March 1, 1889, the Superintendent of Census, with the approval of the Secretary of the Interior, is authorized to fix the rates of compensation to be allowed the enumerators in advance of the enumeration.

Uniform rates will be allowed for the enumeration of deaths occurring during the census year and for names on the supplemental schedules and veterans' special schedule as follows:

Cents.

For each death reported (Schedule No. 5)........................ 2
For each person mentally or physically defective, and for each prisoner, pauper, or homeless child enumerated (Supplemental Schedules Nos. 1 to 8) 5
For each surviving person or widow of person, who had served in the army, navy, or marine corps of the United States in the war of the rebellion, enumerated (Veterans' Special Schedule) 5

INSTRUCTIONS TO ENUMERATORS. 13

For the return of living persons (Schedule No. 1), of farms (Schedule No. 2), and of establishments of productive industry (Schedule No. 3 and Special Schedules) the rates allowed will be determined according to the varying ease or difficulty of enumeration.

The minimum allowance for each living inhabitant will be 2 cents, for each farm reported 15 cents, and for each manufacturing establishment 20 cents. The minimum rate for living inhabitants will be paid generally in cities and in incorporated towns and villages having a population sufficient to form a separate enumeration district. In certain rural districts higher per capita rates will be allowed, according to the relative sparseness of population, difficulties of travel, and other considerations affecting the matter. In regions where, through sparseness of settlement or other difficulties, it would be impossible for an enumerator to earn fair pay at the maximum per capita rates a per diem allowance has been authorized. The rates of pay of the enumerators of the Tenth Census, and the amounts earned daily by them, have been carefully studied for the various sections of the country, and the inequalities which existed at that census have been eliminated as far as possible.

Each enumerator, before the commencement of the enumeration, will receive from his supervisor a circular announcing the rates of compensation to be paid for his work. At the completion of the enumeration, and after the schedules returned by him have been examined by the supervisor, as required by section 5 of the act of March 1, 1889, a certification of the amount due to each enumerator, in accordance with his returns and the rates authorized for his district, will be made by the supervisor to the Superintendent of Census, and the schedules for such district returned at the same time to the Census Office.

As soon as the schedules are received at the Census Office the statements of the supervisor as to the persons, farms, etc., enumerated will be verified, and vouchers in duplicate sent direct from this office to each enumerator, to be by him receipted in duplicate and returned to the Census Office. Upon the receipt of these vouchers, properly signed, the compensation due to each enumerator will be transmitted by mail in the form of a draft, payable to the order of the enumerator named therein.

SPECIAL INSTRUCTIONS

RELATIVE TO THE ENTRIES TO BE MADE ON THE GENERAL AND SPECIAL SCHEDULES.

In making the entries, whether of names or figures, upon the schedules enumerators must be careful to write clearly and neatly, without interlineations, erasures, or blots, as the original schedules must be returned to the Census Office at Washington for examination and compilation, and are to be finally bound in book form as a permanent record.

Use *black ink* in filling the schedules, and be careful to follow instructions as to the marks and symbols to be used in certain cases. Great care should also be exercised in making the entries upon the proper line and in the proper column. A little heedlessness in this respect may produce the most serious confusion. The schedules have been arranged to help the enumerator to find the proper line and column through the use of dotted, plain, and heavy lines, so that the eye can be guided to find easily the correct place of entry.

The enumerator should also realize the necessity of having every question answered exactly as required by the instructions. In the work of compilation in the Census Office each inquiry is treated as if it were the only one on the schedule, and no reference is made to preceding or following answers. The plainest illustration of this point is the necessity of entering every person who is single as "single," even if it is an infant but a few days old. In counting single persons no reference is made to the age, as shown by a preceding inquiry.

Each schedule is provided with a space for the signature of the enumerator, and each schedule, as soon as filled, must be signed by the enumerator as his certification that the entries contained therein have been wholly made by him. The enumerator is prohibited by law from delegating to any other person his authority to enter dwellings and to interrogate their inhabitants. The work of enumeration must be done by him in person, and can not be performed by proxy. The only exception to this which can arise would be in case the services of an interpreter were necessary, and then only when specially authorized from the Census Office.

16   INSTRUCTIONS TO ENUMERATORS.

SCHEDULE NO. 1.—POPULATION.

The schedule adopted for the enumeration of the population is what is known as the family schedule; that is, a separate schedule for each family, without regard to the number of persons in the family. Three forms of this schedule are provided for the use of enumerators, according as the families to be enumerated are made up of a large or small number of persons.

The single-sheet schedules [7–556a] are provided for use in enumerating families containing from 1 to 10 persons, the double-sheet schedules [7–556b] for use in enumerating families containing more than 10 but not over 20 persons, and the additional sheets [7–556c] for use in enumerating families containing more than 20 persons. In the case of large-families, boarding-houses, lodging-houses, hotels, institutions, schools, etc., containing more than 20 persons use the double sheet for 1 to 20 persons, and such number of the additional sheets as may be necessary. Whenever the additional sheets are used, be careful to write on each sheet, in the spaces provided therefor, the number of the supervisor's district, enumeration district, dwelling-house, and family, and also the name of the institution, school, etc., as the case may be. Also, at the heads of the columns in which the information concerning the several persons enumerated is entered, fill in the "tens" figures on the dotted lines preceding the printed unit figures, and continue to number the columns consecutively, as 21, 22, etc., until all the persons in the family have been enumerated.

Upon one or the other of these forms of the population schedule, according to the size of the family to be enumerated, is to be entered the name of every man, woman, and child who *on the 1st day of June*, 1890, shall have his or her usual place of abode within the enumerator's district. No child born between the 1st day of June, 1890, and the day of the enumerator's visit (say June 5, June 15, etc., as the case may be) is to be entered upon the schedule. On the other hand, every person who was a resident of the district upon the 1st day of June, 1890, but between that date and the day of the enumerator's visit shall have died, should be entered on the schedule precisely as if still living. The object of the schedule is to obtain a list of the inhabitants *on the 1st of June*, 1890, and all changes after that date, whether in the nature of gain or of loss, are to be disregarded in the enumeration.

INSTRUCTIONS TO ENUMERATORS.

In answering the several inquiries on the population and other schedules the space provided for each answer should be filled by a definite statement or a symbol used to denote either that the inquiry is not applicable to the person for whom the answers are being made or that the information can not be obtained. In all cases where the inquiry is not applicable use the following symbol: X. If for any reason it is not possible to obtain answers to inquiries which are applicable to the person enumerated, use the following symbol to denote this fact: =====. The enumerator must bear in mind, however, that where he has every reason to suppose that he can supply the answer himself it is better than the symbol: and in any case the symbol should not be used until he has made every effort to ascertain the proper answer from the persons in the family or in the neighborhood, as required by law.

Illustrative examples of the manner of filling the population schedules and the use of these symbols are contained in printed sheets [7-975] which are supplied to enumerators.

Supervisors' and Enumeration Districts.

The first thing to be entered at the head of each schedule is the number of the supervisor's district and of the enumeration district in which the work is performed. These numbers must be repeated for each family enumerated, and where additional sheets are used these numbers are to be carried to those sheets, as already stated.

Civil Divisions.

Be careful to enter accurately the name of the city, town, township, precinct, etc., and distinguish carefully between the population of villages within townships and the remainder of such townships. The correct enumeration of the population of these minor civil divisions is especially important, and is of interest in the presentation in the printed reports of details concerning these small bodies of population. So far as possible, also, the population of small unincorporated villages and hamlets should be separately reported. Also enter at the head of each schedule, in the spaces provided therefor, the name of the county and state or territory in which the minor subdivision is located. In cities the street, street-number, and ward should be entered in the proper spaces, and in those cities where special sanitary districts have been established for the purposes of the census enumeration the letters used to designate them should be added in some convenient space at the head of each schedule and encircled thus: (A), (B), (C), etc., according to the special letters used to distinguish these sanitary districts.

Institutions.

Wherever an institution is to be enumerated, as a hospital, asylum, almshouse, jail, or penitentiary, the full name and title of the institution should be entered, and all persons having their usual place of abode in such institution, whether officers, attendants, inmates, or persons in confinement, should then be entered consecutively on the schedules as one family. If, as sometimes may be the case, a sheriff, warden, or other prison official may live in one end of the prison building, but separated by a partition wall from the prison proper, his family (including himself as its head) should be returned on a separate schedule, and should not be returned on the schedule upon which the prisoners are entered. Where the officers or attendants, or any of them, do not reside in the institution buildings, but live with their families in detached dwellings, no matter whether the houses are owned by the institution or located in the same grounds, they should be reported on separate schedules, but should be included as a part of the work of the special institution enumerator, where one is appointed, and should not be left to be taken by the district enumerator. It may happen also that some of the officers or attendants may reside wholly outside of the institution precincts, either in rented houses or houses owned by the institution, or by themselves, and in such cases they should be enumerated by the district enumerator and not by the special institution enumerator. The tour of duty of the special institution enumerator should not extend beyond the boundaries of the institution grounds, but should include all those persons and inmates whose usual places of abode are clearly within the territory controlled by the institution.

Persons, Families, and Dwellings.

A.—Number of dwelling-house in the order of visitation.

In the space against the inquiry marked A is to be entered the number of the dwelling-house in the order of visitation. The object of this inquiry is to ascertain the total number of dwelling-houses. A dwelling-house for the purposes of the census means any building or place of abode, of whatever character, material, or structure, in which any person is living at the time of taking the census. It may be a room above a warehouse or factory, a loft above a stable, a wigwam on the outskirts of a settlement, or a dwelling-house in the ordinary sense of that term. A tenement house, whether it contains two, three, or forty families, should be considered for the purposes of the census as one house. A building under one roof suited for two or more families, but with a dividing partition wall and a separate front door for each part of the building, should be counted as two or more houses. A block of houses under one roof, but with separate front doors, should be considered as so many houses, without regard to the number of families in each separate house in the block. Wholly uninhabited dwellings are not to be counted.

B.—Number of families in this dwelling-house.

The inquiry marked B calls for the number of families, whether one or more, in each dwelling-house. *Where there is more than one family in a dwelling-house, this inquiry should be answered only on the schedule for the first family enumerated and omitted on the schedules for the second and subsequent families enumerated in the same house,* to avoid duplication of results; the space on the schedules for the second and subsequent families should be filled, however, by an X, as not being applicable. An example of this character is given on the printed sheets illustrative of the manner of filling schedules.

C.—Number of persons in this dwelling-house.

The inquiry marked C calls for the number of persons in each dwelling-house, and where there is more than one family in the house the answer should represent the total number of persons included in the several families occupying the same house. Where there is but a single family to a house, the answer to this inquiry should be the same as for inquiry E. *Where there is more than one family in a dwelling-house this inquiry, as in the case of inquiry B, should be answered only on the schedule for the first family enumerated.*

D.—Number of family in the order of visitation.

In answer to the inquiry marked D enter the number, in the order of visitation, of each family residing in the district. The

20   INSTRUCTIONS TO ENUMERATORS.

fact that more than one family is often found in a house makes the family number exceed, necessarily, the house number, as called for by inquiry A.

The word family, for the purposes of the census, includes persons living alone, as well as families in the ordinary sense of that term, and also all larger aggregations of people having only the tie of a common roof and table. A hotel, with all its inmates, constitutes but one family within the meaning of this term. A hospital, a prison, an asylum is equally a family for the purposes of the census. On the other hand, the solitary inmate of a cabin, a loft, or a room finished off above a store, and indeed all individuals living out of families, constitute a family in the meaning of the census act.

By "individuals living out of families" is meant all persons occupying lofts in public buildings, above stores, warehouses, factories, and stables, having no other usual place of abode; persons living solitary in cabins, huts, or tents; persons sleeping on river boats, canal boats, barges, etc., having no other usual place of abode, and persons in police stations having no homes. Of the classes just mentioned the most important, numerically, is the first, viz: those persons, chiefly in cities, who occupy rooms in public buildings, or above stores, warehouses, factories, and stables. In order to reach such persons the enumerator will need not only to keep his eyes open to all indications of such casual residence in his enumeration district, but to make inquiry both of the parties occupying the business portion of such buildings and also of the police. In the case, however, of tenement houses and of the so-called "flats" of the great cities as many families are to be recorded as there are separate tables.

A person's home is where he sleeps. There are many people who lodge in one place and board in another; all such persons should be returned as members of that family with which they lodge.

E.—Number of persons in this family.

The answer to this inquiry should correspond to the number of columns filled on each schedule, and care should be taken to have all the members of the family included in this statement and a column filled for each person in the family, including servants, boarders, lodgers, etc. Be sure that the person answering the inquiries thoroughly understands the question, and does not omit any person who should be counted as a member of the family.

INSTRUCTIONS TO ENUMERATORS. 21

Names, Relationship to Head of Family, and whether Survivors of the War of the Rebellion.

1. Christian name in full, initial of middle name, and surname.

Opposite to the inquiry numbered 1 on the schedule are to be entered the names of all persons whose usual place of abode on the 1st day of June, 1890, was in the family enumerated.

The census law furnishes no definition of the phrase "usual place of abode;" and it is difficult, under the American system of a protracted enumeration, to afford administrative directions which will wholly obviate the danger that some persons will be reported in two places and others not reported at all. Much must be left to the judgment of the enumerator, who can, if he will take the pains, in the great majority of instances satisfy himself as to the propriety of including or not including doubtful cases in his enumeration of any given family. In the cases of boarders at hotels or students at schools or colleges the enumerator can by one or two well-directed inquiries ascertain whether the person concerning whom the question may arise has at the time any other place of abode within another district at which he is likely to be reported. Seafaring men are to be reported at their land homes, no matter how long they may have been absent, if they are supposed to be still alive. Hence, sailors temporarily at a sailors' boarding or lodging house, if they *acknowledge any other home within the United States*, are not to be included in the family of the lodging or boarding house. Persons engaged in internal transportation, canal men, expressmen, railroad men, etc., if they habitually return to their homes in the intervals of their occupations, will be reported *as of their families*, and not where they may be temporarily staying on the 1st of June, 1890.

In entering the members of a family the name of the father, mother, or other ostensible head of the family (in the case of hotels, jails, etc., the landlord, jailer, etc.) is to be entered in the first column. It is desirable that the wife should be enumerated in the second column, and the children of the family proper should follow in the order of their ages, as will naturally be the case. The names of all other persons in the family, whether relatives, boarders, lodgers, or servants, should be entered successively in subsequent columns.

The christian name in full and initial of middle name of each person should be first entered and the surname immediately thereunder, as shown in the illustrative example.

2. Whether a soldier, sailor, or marine during the civil war (U. S. or Conf.), or widow of such person.

Write "Sol" for soldier, "Sail" for sailor, and "Ma" for marine. If the person served in the United States forces add "U. S." in parenthesis, and if in the Confederate forces add "Conf." in parenthesis, thus: Sol (U. S.); Sail (U. S.); Sol (Conf.), etc. In the case of a widow of a deceased soldier, sailor, or marine, use the letter "W" in addition to the above designations, as W. Sol (U. S.), W. Sol (Conf.), and so on.

The enumeration of the survivors of the late war, including their names, organizations, length of service, and the widows of such as have died, is to be taken on a special schedule prepared for the purpose, as provided for by the act of March 1, 1889, *and relates only to those persons, or widows of persons, who served in the army, navy, or marine corps of the United States in the late war.* The inquiry concerning the survivors of both the United States and Confederate forces is made on the population schedule so as to ascertain the *number* now living and the *number* who have died and have left widows.

3. Relationship to head of family.

Designate the head of a family, whether a husband or father, widow or unmarried person of either sex, by the word *"Head;"* other members of a family by *wife, mother, father, son, daughter, grandson, daughter-in-law, aunt, uncle, nephew, niece, servant,* or other properly distinctive term, according to the particular relationship which the person bears to the head of the family. Distinguish between *boarders*, who sleep and board in one place, and *lodgers*, who room in one place and board in another. If an inmate of an institution or school, write *inmate, pupil, patient, prisoner*, or some equivalent term which will clearly distinguish inmates from the officers and employés and their families. But all officers and employés of an institution who reside in the institution building are to be accounted, for census purposes, as one family, the head of which is the superintendent, matron, or other officer in charge. If more than one family resides in the institution building, group the members together and distinguish

INSTRUCTIONS TO ENUMERATORS. 23

them in some intelligible way. In addition to defining their natural relationship to the head of the institution or of their own immediate family, their official position in the institution, if any, should be also noted, thus: *Superintendent, clerk, teacher, watchman, nurse*, etc.

Color, Sex, and Age.

4. Whether white, black, mulatto, quadroon, octoroon, Chinese, Japanese, or Indian.

Write *white, black, mulatto, quadroon, octoroon, Chinese, Japanese,* or *Indian*, according to the color or race of the person enumerated. Be particularly careful to distinguish between blacks, mulattoes, quadroons, and octoroons. The word "black" should be used to describe those persons who have three-fourths or more black blood; "mulatto," those persons who have from three-eighths to five-eighths black blood; "quadroon," those persons who have one-fourth black blood; and "octoroon," those persons who have one-eighth or any trace of black blood.

5. Sex.

Write *male* or *female*, as the case may be.

6. Age at nearest birthday. If under one year, give age in months.

Write the age in figures at nearest birthday in whole years, omitting months and days, for each person of one year of age or over. For children who on the 1st of June, 1890, were less than one year of age, give the age in months, or twelfths of a year, thus: $\frac{3}{12}$, $\frac{7}{12}$, $\frac{10}{12}$. For a child less than one month old, state the age as follows: $\frac{0}{12}$. The *exact* years of age for all persons one year old or over should be given whenever it can be obtained. In any event, do not accept the answer "don't know," but ascertain as nearly as possible the approximate age of each person. The general tendency of persons in giving their ages is to use the round numbers, as 20, 25, 30, 35, 40, etc. If the age is given as "about 25," determine, if possible, whether the age should be entered as 24, 25, or 26. Particular attention should be paid to this, otherwise it will be found when the results are aggregated in this office that a much more than normal number of persons have been reported as 20, 25, 30, 35, 40, etc., years of age, and a much less than normal at 19, 21, 24, 26, 29, 31, etc.

Conjugal Condition and Children and Children Living.

7. Whether single, married, widowed, or divorced.

Write *single, married, widowed*, or *divorced*, according to the conjugal condition of the person enumerated. No matter how young the person may be, the conjugal condition, if "single," should be always stated.

8. Whether married during the census year (June 1, 1889, to May 31, 1890).

Write *yes* or *no*, as the case may be.

9. Mother of how many children, and number of these children living.

This inquiry is to be made concerning all women who are or have been married, including those widowed or divorced. The answers should be given in figures, as follows: 6—5; that is, mother of six (6) children, of which five (5) are living. If a woman who is or has been married has had no children, or if none are living, state the fact thus: 0—0 or 3—0, as the case may be.

Place of Birth and Parent Nativity.

10. Place of birth.

Give the place of birth of the *person* whose name appears at the head of the column opposite inquiry 1, and for whom the entries are being made.

11. Place of birth of Father.

Give the place of birth of the *father* of the person for whom the entries are being made.

12. Place of birth of Mother.

Give the place of birth of the *mother* of the person for whom the entries are being made.

If the person (Inquiry 10), or father (Inquiry 11), or mother (Inquiry 12) were born in the United States, name the state or territory, or if of foreign birth name the country. The names of *countries*, and not of cities, are wanted. In naming the country of foreign birth, however, do not write, for instance, "Great Britain," but give the particular country, as *England, Scotland*, or *Wales*.

INSTRUCTIONS TO ENUMERATORS. 23

If the person, or father, or mother were born in a foreign country of American parents, write the name of the country and also the words *American Citizen*. If born at sea, write the words *At Sea;* if in the case of the father or mother the words "At Sea" be used, add the nationality of the father's father or mother's father.

If born in Canada or Newfoundland, write the word "English" or "French" after the particular place of birth, so as to distinguish between persons born in any part of British America of French and English extraction respectively. *This is a most important requirement, and must be closely observed in each case and the distinction carefully made.*

Naturalization.

Inquiries 13, 14, and 15 should be made concerning only those adult *males* of foreign birth who are 21 years of age or over.

13. Number of years in the United States.

Give the answer in figures, as 1, 2, 3, 6, 10, etc., according to the number of years such person (as stated above) may have resided in the United States.

14. Whether naturalized.

Write *yes* or *no*, as the case may be.

15. Whether naturalization papers have been taken out.

If naturalized (Inquiry 14), use the symbol **X**; if not naturalized, (Inquiry 14), write *yes* or *no*, as the case may be, in answer to this inquiry (15).

Profession, Trade, or Occupation, and Months Unemployed.

16. Profession, trade, or occupation.

This is a most important inquiry. Study these instructions closely, and in reporting occupations avoid the use of unmeaning terms. A person's occupation is the profession, trade, or branch of work upon which he chiefly depends for support, and in which he would ordinarily be engaged during the larger part of the year. General or indefinite terms which do not indicate the kind of work done by each person must not be used. You are under no obligation to give a person's occupation just as he expresses it. If he can not tell intelligibly what he *is*, find out what he *does*, and describe his occupation accordingly. The name of the place worked in or article made or worked upon should not be used as the sole basis of the statement of a person's occupation. Endeavor to ascertain always *the character of the service rendered or kind of work done*, and so state it.

The illustrations given under each of the general classes of occupation show the nature of the answers which should be made to this inquiry. They are not intended to cover all occupations, but are indicative of the character of the answers desired in order to secure, for each person enumerated, properly descriptive designations of service rendered or work done by way of occupation and as the means of gaining a livelihood.

Agricultural Pursuits.—Be careful to distinguish between the *farm laborer*, the *farmer*, and *farm overseer;* also between the *plantation laborer*, the *planter*, and *plantation overseer*. These three classes must be kept distinct, and each occupation separately returned.

Do not confuse the *agricultural laborer*, who works on the farm or plantation, with the general or day laborer, who works on the road or at odd jobs in the village or town. Distinguish also between *woodchoppers* at work regularly in the woods or forests and the laborer, who takes a job occasionally at chopping wood.

Make a separate return for *farmers* and *planters* who own, hire, or carry on a farm or plantation, and for *gardeners, fruit growers, nurserymen, florists, vine-growers*, etc., who are engaged in raising vegetables for market or in the cultivation of fruit, flowers, seeds, nursery products, etc. In the latter case, if a man combines two or more of these occupations, be careful to so state it, as *florist, nurseryman and seed-grower*.

Avoid the confusion of the *garden laborer, nursery laborer*, etc., who hires out his services, with the proprietor gardener, florist, nurseryman, etc., who carries on the business himself or employs others to assist him.

Return as *dairymen* or *dairywomen* those persons whose occupation in connection with the farm has to do chiefly with the dairy. Do not confuse them with employés of butter and cheese or condensed milk factories, who should be separately returned by some distinctive term.

INSTRUCTIONS TO ENUMERATORS. 27

Return *stock-herders* and *stock-drovers* separately from *stock-raisers*.

Do not include *lumbermen, raftsmen, log-drivers*, etc., engaged in hauling or transporting lumber (generally by water) from the forest to the mill, with the employes of lumber yards or lumber mills.

Fishing.—For *fishermen* and *oystermen* describe the occupation as accurately as possible. Be careful to avoid the return of fishermen on vessels as sailors. If they gain their living by fishing, they should be returned as "fishermen," and not as sailors.

Mining and Quarrying.—Make a careful distinction between the *coal miners* and *miners of ores;* also between miners generally and *quarrymen*. State the *kind* of ore mined or stone quarried.

Do not return *proprietors* or *officials* of mining or quarrying companies as miners or quarrymen, but state their business or official position accurately.

Professional Pursuits.—This class includes *actors, artists* and *teachers of art, clergymen, dentists, designers, draughtsmen, engravers, civil engineers* and *surveyors, mechanical* and *mining engineers, government clerks* and *officials, journalists, lawyers, musicians* and *teachers of music, physicians, surgeons, professors* (in colleges and universities), *teachers* (in schools), and other pursuits of a professional nature. Specify each profession in detail, according to the fact. These are cited simply as illustrations of these classes of pursuits.

Distinguish between *actors, theatrical managers,* and *showmen*.

Make a separate return for *government clerks* occupying positions under the national, state, county, city, or town governments from clerks in offices, stores, manufacturing establishments, etc.; also distinguish *government officials*.

Return *veterinary surgeons* separately from other surgeons.

Distinguish *journalists, editors,* and *reporters* from *authors* and other *literary persons* who do not follow journalism as a distinct profession.

Return separately *chemists, assayers, metallurgists,* and other scientific persons.

Domestic and Personal Service.—Among this class of occupations are comprised *hotel keepers, boarding-house keepers, restaurant*

28   INSTRUCTIONS TO ENUMERATORS.

keepers, *saloon keepers*, and *bartenders*; *housekeepers*, *cooks*, and *servants* (in hotels, boarding-houses, hospitals, institutions, private families, etc.); *barbers* and *hairdressers*; *city*, *town*, and *general day laborers*; *janitors*, *sextons*, and *undertakers*; *nurses* and *midwives*; *watchmen*, *policemen*, and *detectives*. Specify each occupation or kind of service rendered in detail, according to the fact. The above are given only as examples of the occupations which would naturally be included under this general class of work.

Distinguish carefully between *housekeepers*, or women who receive a stated wage or salary for their services, and *housewives*, or women who keep house for their own families or for themselves, without any gainful occupation. The occupation of grown daughters who assist in the household duties without fixed remuneration should be returned as "*Housework—without pay.*"

As stated under agricultural pursuits, do not confuse *day laborers*, at work for the city, town, or at odd jobs, with the agricultural laborer, at work on the farm or plantation or in the employ of gardeners, nurserymen, etc. State specifically the *kind* of work done in every instance.

Clerks in hotels, restaurants, and saloons should be so described and carefully distinguished from *bartenders*. In many instances bartenders will state their occupation as "clerk" in wine store, etc., but the character of the service rendered by such persons will readily determine whether they should be classed as "bartenders" or not.

Stationary engineers and *firemen* should be carefully distinguished from *engineers* and *firemen* employed on locomotives, steamboats, etc.

Soldiers, *sailors*, and *marines* enlisted in the service of the United States should be so returned. Distinguish between officers and enlisted men, and for civilian employes return the kind of service performed by them.

Pursuits of Trade and Transportation.—Distinguish carefully between *real estate agents*, *insurance agents*, *claim agents*, *commission agents*, etc. If a person is a real estate agent and also an auctioneer, as is often the case, return his occupation as *real estate agent and auctioneer*.

Return accountants, bookkeepers, clerks, cashiers, etc., separately, and state the kind of service rendered, as *accountant*—

INSTRUCTIONS TO ENUMERATORS. 29

insurance; *bookkeeper—wholesale dry goods;* *clerk—gas company;* *cashier—music store.*

Do not confound a clerk with a salesman, as is often done, especially in dry goods stores, grocery stores, and provision stores. Generally speaking, the persons so employed are to be considered as salesmen, unless the bulk of their service is in the office on the books and accounts; otherwise they should be returned as *salesman—dry goods; salesman—groceries,* etc.

Stenographers and *typewriters* should be reported separately, and should not be described simply as "clerks."

Distinguish carefully between *bank clerks, cashiers in banks,* and *bank officials,* describing the particular position filled in each case. In no case should a *bank cashier* be confounded with cashiers in stores, etc.

Distinguish between foremen and overseers, packers and shippers, porters and helpers, and errand, office, and messenger boys in stores, etc., and state in each case the character of the duties performed by them, as *foreman—wholesale wool house; packer— crockery; porter—rubber goods; errand boy—dry goods; messenger boy—telegraph.*

State the kind of merchants and dealers, as *dry goods merchant, wood and coal dealer,* etc. Whenever a single word will express the business carried on, as *grocer,* it should be so stated.

In the case of hucksters and peddlers also state the kind of goods sold, as *peddler—tinware.*

Distinguish *traveling salesmen* from *salesmen* in stores, and state the kind of goods sold by them.

Return *boarding* and *livery-stable keepers* separately from *hostlers* and other stable employés.

Distinguish also between *expressmen, teamsters, draymen,* and *carriage and hack drivers.*

Steam railroad employes should be reported separately, according to the nature of their work, as *baggagemen, brakemen, conductors, laborers on railroad, locomotive engineers, locomotive firemen, switchmen, yardmen,* etc.

Officials of railroad, telegraph, express, and *other companies* should be separately returned and carefully distinguished from the employes of such companies.

Boatmen, canalmen, pilots, longshoremen, stevedores, and *sailors* (on steam or sailing vessels) should be separately returned.

xlii

INSTRUCTIONS TO ENUMERATORS.

Telegraph operators, telephone operators, telegraph linemen, telephone linemen, electric-light men, etc., should be kept distinct, and a separate return made for each class.

Manufacturing and Mechanical Pursuits.—In reporting occupations pertaining to manufactures there are many difficulties in the way of showing the kind of work done rather than the article made or the place worked in. The nature of certain occupations is such that it is well nigh impossible to find properly descriptive terms without the use of some expression relating to the article made or place in which the work is carried on.

Do not accept "maker" of an article or "works in" mill, shop, or factory, but strive always to find out the particular work done.

Distinguish between persons who tend machines and the unskilled workman or laborer in mills, factories, and workshops.

Describe the proprietor of the establishment as a "manufacturer," and specify the branch of manufacture, as *cotton manufacturer*, etc. In no case should a manufacturer be returned as a "maker" of an article.

In the case of apprentices, state the trade to which apprenticed, as *Apprentice—carpenter*, etc.

Distinguish between *butchers*, whose business is to slaughter cattle, swine, etc., and *provision dealers*, who sell meats only.

Distinguish also between a *glover, hatter*, or *furrier* who actually make or make up in their own establishments all or part of the gloves, hats, or furs which they sell, and the person who simply deals in but does not make these articles.

Do not use the words "factory operative," but specify in every instance the kind of work done, as *cotton mill—spinner; silk mill—weaver*, etc.

Do not describe a person in a printing office as a "printer" where a more expressive term can be used, as *compositor, pressman, press feeder*, etc.

Make the proper distinction between a *clock* or *watch* "*maker*" and a *clock* or *watch* "*repairer*." Do not apply the word "jeweler" to those who make watches, watch chains, or jewelry in large establishments.

Avoid in all cases the use of the word "mechanic," and state whether a *carpenter, mason, house painter, machinist, plumber*, etc.

Do not say "finisher," "molder," "polisher," etc., but state the article finished, molded, or polished, as *brass finisher, iron molder, steel polisher,* etc.

Distinguish between *cloak makers, dressmakers, seamstresses, tailoresses,* etc. In the case of *sewing-machine operators,* specify the work done.

Other Occupations.—When a lawyer, merchant, manufacturer, etc., has retired from practice or business, say *retired lawyer, retired merchant,* etc.

The distinction to be made between *housewives, housekeepers,* and those assisting in *housework* has already been stated under "DOMESTIC AND PERSONAL SERVICE." For the large body of persons, particularly young women, who live at home and do nothing, make the return as "No occupation." With respect to infants and children too young to take any part in production or to be engaged in any stated occupation, distinguish between those at home and those attending school. For those too young to go to school, or who for some reason did not attend school during the census year, write the words *At home,* and for those who attended school during some part of the school year write the words, *At school—public,* or *At school—private,* according to the kind of school. If taught by a governess or tutor, it should be so stated. The *student* at college or engaged in special studies should be reported separately from *scholars in public or private schools.*

The doing of domestic errands or family chores out of school hours, where a child regularly attends school, should not be considered an occupation. But if a boy or girl, whatever the age, is earning money regularly by labor, contributing to the family support, or appreciably assisting in mechanical or agricultural industry, the kind of work performed should be stated.

17. Months unemployed during the census year (June 1, 1889, to May 31, 1890).

If a person having a gainful occupation was unemployed during any part of the census year it should be so stated in months and parts of months. If, as may often happen, a person was unemployed at his usual occupation for some time during the census year and yet found other temporary employment for some part or the whole of the time, this fact should be clearly stated. For

32   INSTRUCTIONS TO ENUMERATORS.

instance, a person's occupation may be that of "Farm laborer," at which he may have had no employment for three months during the census year. During two of these three months, however, he may have worked in a shoe shop, so that, so far as actual idleness is concerned, he was only out of work one month. In all such cases, where the non-employment returned in answer to Inquiry 17 does not represent actual idleness as regards the person's usual occupation given in answer to Inquiry 16, indicate the number of months unemployed at occupation by inserting the figures, in parenthesis, after the name of the occupation itself. In the case just cited, and as shown in the "illustrative example," the answer to Inquiry 16 would appear as "Farm laborer (3)" and the answer to Inquiry 17 as "1." For all persons not engaged in gainful occupations the symbol "X" should be used.

School Attendance, Illiteracy, and Language Spoken.

18. **Attendance at school (in months) during the census year (June 1, 1889, to May 31, 1890).**

For all persons between the ages of five and seventeen, inclusive, the attendance at school during the census year should be in all cases stated in months and parts of months. Where a person within the above ages did not attend school at all during the census year write "0," and for all other persons to whom the inquiry is not applicable use the symbol "X."

Inquiries numbered 19 and 20 relate to illiteracy, and are to be made only of or concerning persons ten years of age or over.

19. **Able to read.**

Write *yes* or *no*, as the case may be.

20. **Able to write.**

Write *yes* or *no*, as the case may be.

A person may not be able to read or write the English language and yet may be able to read or write (or both) their native language, as French, Spanish, Italian, etc. If in such cases a person can read or write (or both) some language, the answer to Inquiry 19 and Inquiry 20 should be "yes," according to the fact. If not able to so read or write the answer should be "no." For all persons *under ten* years of age use the symbol "X."

INSTRUCTIONS TO ENUMERATORS. 33

21. Able to speak English. If not, the language or dialect spoken.

This inquiry should also be made of or concerning every person ten years of age or over. If the person is able to speak English so as to be understood in ordinary conversation, write *English;* otherwise, write the name of the language or dialect in which he usually expresses himself, as *German, Portuguese, Canadian French, Pennsylvania Dutch,* etc. For all persons *under* ten years of age use the symbol "**X**."

Mental and Physical Defects, etc.

22. Whether suffering from acute or chronic disease, with name of disease and length of time afflicted.

If a person is suffering from acute or chronic disease so as to be unable to attend to ordinary business or duties, give the name of the disease and the length of time that it has lasted.

23. Whether defective in mind, sight, hearing, or speech, or whether crippled, maimed, or deformed, with name of defect.

If a person is mentally or physically defective, state the nature of the defect.

24. Whether a prisoner, convict, homeless child, or pauper.

If the person is a prisoner, convict, homeless child, or pauper, be careful to so state, as "*prisoner*," "*pauper*," etc.

25. Supplemental schedule and page.

If answers are required to Inquiries 22, 23, or 24, indicate in this space the number of the Supplemental Schedule and page of schedule on which the special inquiries relating to such person have been answered. (See instructions concerning Supplemental Schedules.)

Ownership of Homes and Farms.

26. Is the home you live in hired, or is it owned by the head or by a member of the family?

If hired, say *Hired;* if owned, say *Owned,* and indicate whether owned by *head, wife, son, daughter,* or other member of family, as *Owned—head; Owned—wife; Owned—son,* etc. If there is more than one son or daughter in the family, and the home is owned by one of them, indicate which one by using the figure at the head of the column in which the name, etc., of the person is entered, as *Owned—son* (4).

27. **If owned by head or member of family, is the home free from mortgage incumbrance?**

If free from incumbrance, say *Free;* if mortgaged, say *Mortgaged.*

28. **If the head of family is a farmer, is the farm which he cultivates hired, or is it owned by him or by a member of his family?**

To be answered in the same manner as for Inquiry 26.

29. **If owned by head or member of family, is the farm free from mortgage incumbrance?**

To be answered in the same manner as for Inquiry 27.

30. **If the home or farm is owned by head or member of family, and mortgaged, give the post-office address of owner.**

In answer to this inquiry the post-office address of the owner of a *mortgaged* home or farm must be correctly stated; that is, the post-office at which the owner (whether head of family, wife, son, daughter, etc.) usually receives his or her mail.

In all cases where it can not be definitely ascertained whether the home or farm is mortgaged or not return the post-office address of the owner, so that this office can communicate with such persons.

In connection with the definition of mortgage incumbrance it should be stated that judgment notes or confessions of judgment, as in Pennsylvania and Virginia, the deeds of trust of many states, deeds with vendor's lien clause, bonds or contracts for title that are virtually mortgages, crop liens or mortgages upon crops, and all other legal instruments that partake of the nature of mortgages upon real estate, are to be regarded as such; but mechanics' liens are not to be regarded as mortgage incumbrances upon homes or farms.

The enumerator should be careful to use the local name for the mortgage incumbrance when making the inquiries, and should not confine himself to the word "mortgage" when it will be misunderstood.

Some of the difficulties which will arise in connection with the prosecution of the inquiries concerning homes and farms, and how they are to be treated, may be mentioned, as follows:

1. A house is not necessarily to be considered as identical with

INSTRUCTIONS TO ENUMERATORS. 35

a home and to be counted only once as a home. If it is occupied as a home by one or more tenants, or by owner and one or more tenants, it is to be regarded as a home to each family.

2. If a person owns and cultivates what has been two or more farms and lives on one, they are not to be taken as more than one farm.

3. If a person owns and cultivates what has been two or more farms and all are not mortgaged, the several farms are to be counted as one farm and as mortgaged.

4. If a person hires both the farm he cultivates and the home he lives in, or owns both, the home is to be considered as a part of the farm.

5. If a person owns the home he lives in and hires the farm he cultivates, or owns the farm he cultivates and hires the home he lives in, both farm and home are to be entered upon the schedule, and separately.

6. If the tenant of a farm and its owner live upon it, either in the same house or in different houses, the owner is to be regarded as owning the home he lives in and the tenant as hiring the farm he cultivates. If the owner simply boards with the tenant no account is to be made of the owner.

7. If the same person owns and cultivates one farm and hires and cultivates another farm, he is to be entered upon the schedule as owning the farm he cultivates.

8. The head of a family may own and cultivate a farm and his wife may own another farm which is let to tenant, perhaps to her husband. In such case only the farm which is owned by the head of the family is to be considered, but the rented farm is to be taken account of when its tenant's family is visited.

9. A person who cultivates a farm is not to be regarded as hiring it if he works for a definite and fixed compensation in money or fixed quantity of produce, but he is to be regarded as hiring it if he pays a rental for it or is to receive a share of the produce, even though he may be subject to some direction and control by the owner.

SCHEDULE NO. 2.—AGRICULTURE.

"Farms" for the purposes of the agricultural schedule include, besides what are commonly known as farms, all considerable nurseries, orchards, and market gardens owned by separate parties, which are cultivated for pecuniary profit, and employ as much as the labor of one able-bodied workman during the year. Mere cabbage and potato patches, family vegetable gardens, and ornamental lawns, not constituting a portion of a farm for general agricultural purposes, will be excluded. No farm will be reported of less than three acres unless five hundred dollars' worth of produce has been actually sold from it during the year. The latter proviso will allow the inclusion of many market gardens in the neighborhood of large cities, where, although the area is small, a high state of cultivation is maintained and considerable values are produced.

A farm is what is owned or leased by one man and cultivated under his care. A distant wood-lot or sheep-pasture, even if in another subdivision or district, is to be treated as a part of the farm; but wherever there is a resident overseer or a manager there a separate farm is to be reported.

The amounts of the various crops may be estimated according to the best judgment of the proprietor or manager where no exact account is kept.

Special instructions as to certain inquiries are contained on the schedule. Those instructions and the following additional explanations should receive the careful attention of all enumerators.

Improved or *unimproved land* should be carefully noted. All land once plowed is *improved* unless afterward abandoned for cultivation, like the "old fields" of the South. Western enumerators will pay special attention to this instruction, and not be guided by local customs. Rocky, hill, and mountain pastures are *not improved*, but fields used for pasture as a part of a rotation of crops *are* improved.

Weeks of hired labor should be obtained by adding together the number of weeks *each* individual of the help employed was at work, thus: one man hired by the year should be counted as 52 weeks; another man for twenty-six weeks as 26 weeks; two men in hay and in harvest each six weeks as 12 weeks, and one woman in the dairy for a year as 52 weeks; making a total for that farm of 142 weeks of hired labor.

Farmers should be encouraged to give as full and complete answers to the various questions as possible, and the fact should be impressed upon them that they, above all others, are interested in having the returns of the census as near the truth as it is possible to get them.

SCHEDULE NO. 3 AND SPECIAL SCHEDULES.—MANUFACTURES.

The following schedules are provided for the collection of the statistics of manufactures:

GENERAL SCHEDULE NO. 3 [7-560].

To be used to report establishments whose operations do not come within the scope of either of the special schedules.

SPECIAL SCHEDULES.

No. 1. Agricultural Implements.
No. 2. Paper Mills.
No. 3. Boots and Shoes. (Not including custom work and repairing, which should be returned on General Schedule No. 3.)
No. 4. Leather, Tanned and Curried.
No. 5. Lumber Mills and Saw Mills. (Including their remanufactures. Planing mills and sash, door, and blind factories separately conducted should be returned on General Schedule No. 3.) Timber products not produced by lumber mills and saw mills must be separately returned on Special Schedule No. 5 a.
No. 6. Brick Yards.
No. 7. Flour and Grist Mills.
No. 8. Cheese, Butter, and Condensed Milk Factories. (Not including farm products, which should be returned by enumerators on Schedule No. 2—Agriculture.)
No. 9. Slaughtering and Meat Packing. (Not including retail butchering establishments.)
No. 10. Chemical Manufactures.
No. 11. Clay and Pottery Products.
No. 12. Coke. (Not to be taken by enumerators.)
No. 13. Cotton Manufactures.
No. 14. Dyeing and Finishing of Textiles.
No. 15. Electrical Industry. (Not to be taken by enumerators.)
No. 16. Glass. (Not to be taken by enumerators.)
No. 17. Manufactured Gas. (Not to be taken by enumerators.)
No 18. Iron and Steel. (Not to be taken by enumerators.)
No. 19. Printing, Publishing, and the Periodical Press.

INSTRUCTIONS TO ENUMERATORS.

No. 20. Shipbuilding.
No. 21. Silk and Silk Goods.
No. 22. Wool Manufactures.
No. 23. Hosiery and Knit Goods.
No. 24. Carriages and Wagons.
No. 25. Salt Works. (Not to be taken by enumerators.)
No. 26. Leather, Patent, Enameled, and Morocco.

Of the foregoing special schedules the following will be mailed direct from the Census Office to the manufacturers before the time for beginning the enumeration, with the request that the schedules be properly filled out ready for the enumerator when he calls:

No. 2. Paper Mills.
No. 10. Chemical Manufactures.
No. 11. Clay and Pottery Products.
No. 13. Cotton Manufactures.
No. 14. Dyeing and Finishing of Textiles.
No. 20. Shipbuilding.
No. 21. Silk and Silk Goods.
No. 22. Wool Manufactures.
No. 23. Hosiery and Knit Goods.
No. 26. Leather, Patent, Enameled, and Morocco.

In the event that it shall be found by the enumerator that an establishment of the character noted above has not received a schedule upon which to make its return, the enumerator must at once report the fact to the supervisor of his district, in order that the schedule may be forwarded to be filled and taken up by the enumerator before the completion of his work.

The statistics of iron and steel, of coke, of glass, of the electrical industry, of manufactured gas, and of salt will be collected by expert special agents without regard to locality. Enumerators will not visit establishments of these classes.

In cities and towns of importance as manufacturing centers without regard to population the collection of the general statistics of manufactures has been entirely withdrawn from the enumerators and the duty assigned to special agents appointed for each city or town of this class.

A list of the cities and towns in which the collection of these statistics has been withdrawn from the enumerators in each supervisor's district will be furnished the supervisor in order that enu-

INSTRUCTIONS TO ENUMERATORS. 39

merators may be properly instructed in this respect. To guard against possible failure to collect the statistics of these establishments in localities for which special agents are not to be appointed, enumerators, in the absence of specific instructions from the supervisors, should ascertain beyond the possibility of a doubt whether or not they are to enumerate the establishments of productive industry in their respective districts.

In the rural districts, and in cities and towns for which no special agents are to be appointed, as set forth in the preceding paragraph, the statistics of manufactures will be collected by the enumerators appointed to collect the statistics of population and agriculture and during the progress of the work of enumerating the inhabitants.

It is for the information and guidance of enumerators with respect to this duty that these special instructions are provided.

Enumerators shall personally visit each establishment of productive industry, except those above noted, within their respective districts, and obtain upon the proper schedule a return of the operations of such establishment during the census year, June 1, 1889, to May 31, 1890; in the case, however, of establishments whose books of accounts are balanced at a different date, the return may be for the fiscal year of the establishment most nearly conforming to the census year.

The term "Establishment of Productive Industry" must be understood in its broadest sense to embrace not only mills and factories, but also the operations of all small establishments and the mechanical trades, as *blacksmithing, coopering, masonry and bricklaying, mechanical dentistry, wheelwrighting,* etc.

Restaurants, saloons, and barber shops, the compounding of individual prescriptions by druggists and apothecaries, the operations of retail mercantile establishments, transportation corporations and lines, and professional services (except mechanical dentistry, as above noted) are not considered as coming within the meaning of the law in this connection. In case it shall be claimed by any person engaged in the lines of business herein exempt from enumeration that the operations of his establishment are in the nature of productive industry, the facts, together with proper explanatory notes, shall be reported at once to this office through the supervisor of census.

Great care must be taken by enumerators to guard against the

INSTRUCTIONS TO ENUMERATORS.

omission from their returns of any establishment that comes properly within the scope of their investigation. They should have their eyes open to every indication of the presence of productive industry, and should supplement personal observation by frequent and persistent inquiry.

In the event of an establishment located in one enumeration district having an office located in another enumeration district at which the desired information is to be obtained, the enumerator in whose district the establishment is located shall report the facts at once to this office through the supervisor, with such explanation as may be necessary to insure the procurement of a return of the operations of such establishment.

In filling page 1 and question 1, page 3, of the general and special schedules enumerators should be careful to insert correctly the name and address of the corporation, firm, or individual carrying on the business, and with sufficient fullness to enable the Census Office to conduct such subsequent correspondence as may be necessary.

In question 3, general schedule, the kind of business and character of product should be described as specifically as possible, as, for example, "fishing hooks," "hoisting apparatus," "skirt supporters," "speaking tubes," "building hardware," "toys," "fireworks," etc. General terms should be avoided where specific and technical terms will more clearly express the character of the product. Attention is called to the explanatory notes printed on the general and special schedules for manufactures.

It is not necessary to explain at length the use of the word "materials" in respect to manufactures. It will be enough to say that what is the product of one establishment often becomes the material of another, as the product of the foundry may become the material of the machine shop, or the product of the furnace may become the material of the forge and mill, or the product of the woolen mill may become the material of the clothing manufacturer.

The cost of materials and values of products must be reported for all establishments returned upon the general or special schedules. Care must be taken to report clearly and fully (question 7) the kinds, quantities, and cost of the more important materials used by each establishment, and to report in like manner (question 8) the kinds, quantities, and values of the

INSTRUCTIONS TO ENUMERATORS. 41

principal products. The kinds and quantities of materials and products noted in the questions on the special schedules must be reported in detail for all establishments returned upon either of such special schedules.

Care should be taken to assure manufacturers that the details of their business will not be made public or communicated to any but authorized employes of the Census Office. The returns of manufacturing establishments will be used only for the purposes of tabulation, and no publication will be made in the census reports that will disclose the operations of individual establishments. This assurance is set forth on each schedule over the signature of the Superintendent of Census.

SCHEDULE NO. 5.—MORTALITY.

Special instructions for filling this schedule [7-417] are printed on the schedule itself, and need not be repeated here.

In certain cities and localities Schedule No. 5 has been withdrawn from the enumerators, as authorized by section 18 of the act of March 1, 1889, and the supervisors have been instructed to so inform the enumerators. All other enumerators not so informed will make the inquiries, as provided for on Schedule No. 5.

In the following states there is a more or less complete local registration of deaths which gives, in almost all cases, the name, age, and sex of those who have died, but does not give certain other items which are called for in the mortality schedule:

Alabama, Connecticut, Massachusetts, Minnesota, New Hampshire, New Jersey, New York, Rhode Island, and Vermont.

In these states the enumerators from whom the schedules are not withdrawn are advised and instructed to consult these local records for the purpose of making their lists of deaths complete as to number; and if they can arrange to copy the names, sex, and age from the local records before starting on their rounds they will then find it easy to fill out the data called for on the mortality schedules.

In all the states many towns and cities from 5,000 to 15,000 inhabitants have a local registration of deaths which is more or less complete, and in all places where such local registration exists the enumerators should consult the records and, if possible, obtain lists of names, with age and sex, to aid them in their work of obtaining a complete record of deaths.

In the following cities special sanitary districts have been created and the enumerators' districts arranged with reference to keeping the population of each of these sanitary districts distinct: Allegheny City, Baltimore, Boston, Brooklyn, Buffalo, Charleston, Chicago, Cincinnati, Cleveland, District of Columbia, Kansas City, Minneapolis, Nashville, New Orleans, New York City, Philadelphia, Pittsburgh, Saint Louis, Saint Paul, San Francisco, and Yonkers.

The letter used to designate each sanitary district should be entered on the population, mortality, and supplemental schedules in every instance.

SUPPLEMENTAL SCHEDULES.

In addition to the general schedules for population, agriculture, and manufactures, already described, there are eight supplemental schedules which call for special information concerning the insane, feeble-minded and idiotic, deaf, blind, those diseased and physically defective (not otherwise enumerated), children in benevolent institutions, prisoners, and paupers, as follows:

No. 1.—Statistics of Insanity.
No. 2.—Statistics of Feeble-mindedness and Idiocy.
No. 3.—Statistics of the Deaf.
No. 4.—Statistics of the Blind.
No. 5.—Statistics of Persons Diseased and Physically Defective.
No. 6.—Statistics of Benevolence.
No. 7.—Statistics of Crime.
No. 8.—Statistics of Pauperism.

Each person belonging to the several classes indicated above is to be entered first upon the regular population schedule, with all the particulars required in the case of any inhabitant. This information is to be transferred to the supplemental schedule of his class, as explained on the schedules themselves, and in addition make the special inquiries called for on each supplemental schedule. For each person thus entered on the supplemental schedule the enumerator will receive additional compensation and at higher rates (5 cents for each name) than for entries upon the regular population schedule.

In transferring to the supplemental schedule the answers to certain inquiries on the population schedule it will be necessary to use abbreviations, owing to the width of the columns, as follows:

3. Write *Hd,* for head of family; *Wfe,* for wife; *Son; Dau,* for

INSTRUCTIONS TO ENUMERATORS. 43

daughter; *Gd-son*, for grandson; *Gd-dau*, for granddaughter; *Dau-in-law*, for daughter-in-law; *Aunt*; *Unc*, for uncle; *Neph*, for nephew; *Niece*; *Svt*, for servant; *Bdr*, for boarder; *Ldgr*, for lodger. Write *Inm*, for inmate; *Pu*, for pupil; *Pat*, for patient; *Pr*, for prisoner.

4. Write *W*, for white; *B*, for black; *Mu*, for mulatto; *Qd.* for quadroon; *Oc*, for octoroon; *Ch*, for Chinese; *Jp*, for Japanese; *In*, for Indian.

5. Write *M*, for male; *F*, for female.

7. Write *Sg*, for single; *Mr*, for married; *Wd*, for widow; *Dv*, for divorced.

Under "Physical defects" write *yes* in the column or columns indicating the particular defect or defects reported, except in "defective speech," which is to be answered as indicated in the inquiry itself.

In all other respects the answers as made on the population schedule can be transferred without abbreviation to the spaces provided on the supplemental schedules.

The nature of the information called for by these supplemental schedules is fully explained upon the schedules themselves.

Enumerators will take notice that the persons enumerated on the supplemental schedules, whether in or out of institutions, may belong to more than one of the special classes. For example, the pauper insane in hospitals and asylums for the insane are to be enumerated both as insane and as paupers, and all the questions contained on both of these schedules are to be filled, in order that they may be in proper shape for the work to be done upon them in the Census Office when received. The same remark applies to insane prisoners, to deaf or blind children in orphan schools or in homes for the friendless, and in many similar cases. A full description is to be made of each person belonging to more than one of the special classes on each of the schedules for each of the classes to which he belongs. For this double work double pay will be allowed.

Some of the questions contained on the supplemental schedules can not be answered by means of a personal interview with each person so enumerated, but can be answered by examination of the institution records, if in an institution. In all such cases it will be expected and required that the enumerator shall examine the records and reply to each special question as fully as may be possible.

44   INSTRUCTIONS TO ENUMERATORS.

Wherever there is a city or town lock-up in which prisoners are retained usually for but a single night or a night and a day the enumerator will be expected to visit it on the first Monday of June, to ascertain whether there are any prisoners then in confinement in it, and not to delay such visit until a later date.

Enumerators should understand that the object of the inquiry relating to paupers is to ascertain the number of persons who were on the first day of June wholly or partly, but permanently, supported at the expense of the poor fund belonging to any state, county, city, or town. From this class should be excluded all persons not inmates of almshouses who receive only temporary aid at their homes. But all inmates of almshouses should be reported on the pauper schedule, also those not in almshouses who are boarded out at public expense or kept on any private farm or in any private house at public expense. In every enumeration district an effort should be made, in advance of entering upon the work of enumeration, to find out, if the enumerator does not already know, whether any county or town paupers are kept for pay by any of the inhabitants of the district, and all such should be reported, subject to the caution given above.

Care must be exercised in the case of every almshouse, lock-up, police station, jail, prison, hospital, asylum, school, or other institution to write the name of the institution in full at the top of each page of the general and supplemental schedules.

SPECIAL SCHEDULE.—SURVIVING SOLDIERS, ETC.

The provision of the act of March 1, 1889, under which the special enumeration of survivors of the war of the rebellion is made, reads as follows:

That said Superintendent shall, under the authority of the Secretary of the Interior, cause to be taken on a special schedule of inquiry, according to such form as he may prescribe, the names, organizations, and length of service of those who had served in the Army, Navy, or Marine Corps of the United States in the war of the rebellion, and who are survivors at the time of said inquiry, and the widows of soldiers, sailors, or marines.

The entries concerning each survivor or widow should be carefully and accurately made, so that the printed reports may contain only thoroughly trustworthy information.

Spaces are provided on the special schedule for the entry of fifty names, or, more properly, terms of service. The spaces are numbered consecutively from 1 to 50, and cover the four pages comprised

INSTRUCTIONS TO ENUMERATORS. 45

in each schedule. The inquiries made concerning each survivor or widow call for the repetition of the number of the house and family as returned on the general Population Schedule (No. 1), the name, rank, company, regiment, or vessel, date of enlistment, date of discharge, and length of service (in years, months, and days) on the upper half of each page, and the post-office address, disability incurred, and general remarks on the lower half of each page. The column headed "Remarks" is intended to be used to cover any points not included in the foregoing inquiries and which are necessary to a complete statement of a person's term of service.

In the case of persons having served in more than one organization, use as many spaces as may be necessary to cover their various terms of service.

In the case of widows of deceased soldiers, sailors, or marines, make the entry of her name on the dotted line, as follows: Lucretia A., widow of ——————————— Ashton, John R. filling out the record of his service during the war, and giving under "Post-office address" the present address of the widow.

Where a person enlisted under an assumed name, and was so borne on the muster-rolls, but who has since resumed his lawful name, and under which he would be enumerated on the population schedule, make the entry on the special schedule for survivors as follows: John H. Brown, alias ———————————— Galbreath, James H.

In this case the man's real name is John H. Brown, but the name under which he served was James H. Galbreath.

The attention of enumerators is called specially to the fact that from a number of the states there were *two*, and in some instances *three*, and even *four* regiments mustered into the service of the United States at different dates during the war whose designations were the same or so nearly similar as to be easily confounded with each other. For example: In Massachusetts the Sixth Regiment of Infantry was organized in August and September, 1862, to serve nine months, and was mustered out June 3, 1863; the Sixth Regiment of Militia Infantry was organized April 22, 1861, to serve three months, and was mustered out in July, 1861, and the Sixth Regiment of Militia Infantry was organized in July, 1864, to serve one hundred days, and was mustered out October 27, 1864. So also there were two organizations from that state—among several similar duplications—called the Second Unattached Company Militia Infantry: one organized May 3, 1864, to serve ninety days, and mustered out August 6, 1864, and the other organized August 7, 1864, to serve one hundred days, and mustered out November 15, 1864. In Ohio the Sixtieth Infantry (one year's service) was organized in February, 1862, and mustered out November 10, 1862 and the Sixtieth Infantry (three years' service) was organized in the months of February, March, April, and May, 1864, and mustered out July 28, 1865. The Eighty-eighth Infantry (three months' service) was organized in June, 1862, and mustered out September 26, 1862, and the Eighty-eighth Infantry (three years' service) was organized from September 24, 1862, to August 3, 1863, and was mustered out July 3, 1865. In Missouri the First Regiment Infantry was organized in April and May, 1861, to serve three months; two companies were mustered out in July and August, 1861, and the remaining companies reorganized for three years' service, and the designation changed to the First Missouri Light Artillery September 1, 1861; the First Regiment U. S. Reserve Corps, Missouri, was organized May 7, 1861, to serve three months, and mustered out August 20, 1861; the First Regiment U. S. Reserve Corps, Missouri, was organized September 3–14, 1861, to serve during the war in Missouri, and mustered out in September and October, 1862; and the First Regiment (state militia) was organized from December, 1861, to May, 1862, to serve during the war in Missouri, and mustered out by companies from December, 1864, to May, 1865. In Pennsylvania the Twentieth Regiment Volunteer Infantry was organized April 30, 1861, to serve three months, and was mustered out August 6, 1861; and the Twentieth Regiment Militia Infantry was organized June 17, 1863, to serve during the emergency, and mustered out August 10, 1863.

Enumerators should also be careful to distinguish between the *arms* of the service, and in giving the record of the service of a soldier state whether he belonged, for example, to the Cavalry, Artillery (heavy or light), Engineers, or Infantry.

All men *who were mustered into the military service of the United States during the late war* should be enumerated.

Superintendent of Census.

MISCELLANEOUS PHOTOGRAPHS

PINE RIDGE AGENCY
PINE RIDGE SOUTH DAKOTA

The following illustration names are within this set or are a party with a family name or relation of the same; or the photograph itself was taken at or near Pine Ridge.

Photographer: Edward S. Curtis, 1868-1952 (ca 1910 Dec. 8)

Cheyenne young woman

Photographer: Heyn & Matzen, Chicago (ca 1900)

Eagle Feather and baby (Sioux)

Photographer: Unknown (ca 1908)

Iron Shell, Lakota Sioux

Photographer: Heyn & Matzen, Chicago (ca 1900 May 24)

John Lone Bull
Sioux Indian child holding bow and arrows

Photographer: W.R. Cross' Studio (ca 1907)

Indian woman and small child
Pine Ridge Agency

Photographer: Frances Benjamin Johnston, 1864-1952 (1897)

Seven Sioux children before entering school

Photographer: Unknown (1879)

Sioux boys as they arrived at the Indian Training School at Carlisle Barracks, Oct. 5, 1879

Photographer: Adolph F. Muhr, -1913 (1899)

White Face, Sioux man, wearing a breast plate and animal hide sash with medallions and holding a long handled war club.

Photographer: Richard Throssel, 1933 (ca 1907)

A Cheyenne warrior of the future with full headdress and holding a rifle.

Photographer: John C.H. Grabill (1891)

A young Oglala girl sitting in front of a tipi, with a puppy beside her, probably on or near Pine Ridge Reservation.